You Are Not Defeated

by
Amana-Johari Allen

authorHOUSE®

AuthorHouse™
1663 Liberty Drive, Suite 200
Bloomington, IN 47403
www.authorhouse.com
Phone: 1-800-839-8640

First published by AuthorHouse 3/31/2008

ISBN: 978-1-4343-7068-6 (sc)

Printed in the United States of America
Bloomington, Indiana

Dedication

First I would like to give an honor to God who has instilled in me the gift of poetry. This book was written to encourage everyone who feels that they can not make it through the storms of life. He has allowed me to endure many obstacles and because of my endurance and faith I am able to put my triumph into poetry to encourage others to keep the faith. This book is dedicated to everyone who has ever believed in me and had envisioned my potential before I did thank you; and especially to those of you who have played a part in my life inspiring the words that I have written. I love you and may the Lord bless you and keep you in His unchanging hands.

To my husband Ray Henry; thank you for supporting and believing in me. Thanks for having patience especially during the times when you did not understand me I am elated that you now understand that my actions are by Gods grace. To my children mommy loves you and thanks for cheering me on and giving me big smiles when I would perform on stage. To my "Da-De" Arthur I love you and thank you for encouraging me my entire life you have always been there as long as I can remember and it has paid off. To my "big" brother Asante I love you and thanks for always being a big brother to me.

To my mom Denese thank you for supporting me in this journey that I am on. To Arthur Lee Smith thank you for supporting me and for the "small talk".

Acknowledgements

I give special thanks to all of the members of the Pillar of Truth Church of God in Christ. You all are beautiful and I thank you for supporting, encouraging, and believing in me I love all of you. Sister Chris Studway I am sorry for losing your poem and I thank you whole heartedly for obeying God. To Sister Kysha Jackson thank you for sticking this out with me you involved yourself as though it were you.

And I thank God for our Pastor Ben Brown who is an awesome man of God. Pastor you always obey God and you are always led by Him in your actions I truly respect and appreciate you as a pastor, father, brother and friend in Christ an awesome leader you are. To our First Lady Alberta Brown thank you for the on going encouraging words and smiles the warm hugs and calls of concern.

I would like to thank the Take It by Force Ministries Pastor Steven Bozeman for accepting the many phone calls and helping me to warfare my way through this journey. Pastor you are such an obedient man of God the brotherly understanding that you have for us is remarkable you take it straight into warfare. To Marlene Snipes a very loyal person who is always on fire for the Lord I love you. To my "special" sister in Christ Benita Moore I love you. You were there with me through this entire warfare you even told me that I would write this book when I said that I wouldn't. Thank you for being obedient to God you truly were and are a blessing in my life. To Latasha Parrish my other big sister I love you more than words could say you were there as well to endure these trials. Thanks for always keeping it real. To Yvonne my Spiritual mom, friend, and confidant thank you, thank you, and thank you.

Acknowledgements

I would like to thank the staff and students at West Wood College you all are great thank you for believing in me.

Jimmie Blackburn (student)

Valencia Burton (student)

Lanessa Hernton (student)

Richard Holloway (staff)

Sylvia D. James (R.I.P) (staff)

Danielle Land (staff)

Theodore Lyons (staff)

Ahmed Nickerson (staff)

Shirley Oliphant (staff)

Paul Phelps*(student)

Lindsay Schultz (staff)

Mechelle Smith (staff)

Regina Vereen (staff)

I would like to give a huge thanks to the parents and staff of Legacy Charter School you all have encouraged me on a daily basis and I appreciate that. Special thanks to Shuna Price, Kevin and Wendy (Mrs. M) McLaughlin you all were a blessing in disguise. Ms. Lisa Kenner thank you so much for always having an open ear and heart and thank you for always putting me on the "front line" helping me to overcome my fear of public speaking.

Sincere thanks to Author House and my publishing consultant Elaine Headley- Jerome thank you for not forgetting about me.

Contents

1 Timothy 3:15

But if I tarry long, that thou mayest know how thou oughest to behave thyself in the house of God, which is the church of the living God, the pillar and ground of the truth.

The Pillar of Truth

You taught me how to praise the Lord; you taught me how to stay
saved
You taught me that God is with us on every hand, you taught me
that the devil only comes to kill, steal, and destroy
You taught me that this battle was already won
You taught me to hold my tongue that peace may be still; you
taught me that we live because of God's will
You taught me that if my testimony is true that heaven belongs to
me
And that regardless of what I do Satan belongs beneath my feet
You teach me the scriptures as if you wrote them yourself, while
reassuring me to call on the Lord for help
"Be wise as serpents and humble as doves" and in all that I do
acknowledge the Lord
I feel honored to be a member of the body of Christ
And I wish that I understood completely a long time ago what it
meant to give the Lord my life
I have grown to realize that it is all in Gods speed
This poem was written to the Pillar of Truth from me.

James 5:16

Confess your faults one to another, and pray one for another, that ye may be healed. The effectual fervent prayer of a righteous man availeth much.

Confessions Of The Ten Commandments

Our father which are in heaven hallow be thy name
I come to you with my hands up high for I have committed sin
Adultery, fornication, and told a web of lies, disobeyed my parents
and took what wasn't mine
Caused someone to breathe no more and used your name in vain
I wanted what the Jones's had and I worked on the Sabbath day
I have idoled some of the greatest rappers known to man and I
made the devil dance on Halloween
Lord you said "Confess our faults one to another that we may be
healed"
so I have spoken the truth and would like my heart to be filled
Thank you Lord for blessing me when I thought I had no friends
Thank you Lord for loving me when I didn't love myself it is
because of you why I still have my health
Thank you Lord for who you are in my life because without you I
could not see, that Satan himself wants to take control of me
So if you know that you're still here on earth because of his will,
then take this time and open your mouth and thank him while you
can.

2 Corinthians 3:14

But their minds were blinded for until this day remained the same vail untaken away in the reading of the Old Testament; which vail is done away in Christ.

The Perfect Storm

The perfect storm is the one you can't see usually the one when you say how can this be
 Your mind is captured in your body and your spirit is totally free
I am not judging you so please don't judge me
 Lift your hands with me let's pray and ask God to forgive because you and I both know that it is for him we want to live
 but in return there is something that we must give
 usually it's something that we think we can't live without
keep your faith strong in the Lord and he will show up without a doubt
 we all must go through trials and tribulations and through this is where we get our lesson
 just continue to walk with God and you will find your blessing and always remember He never stops testing.

James 5:12

But above all things , my brethren, swear not, neither by heaven, neither by heaven, neither by earth, neither by any oath: but let your yea be yea and your nay be nay: lest ye fall into condemnation.

Remember Who You Are

No matter what you do in life and no matter where you do it
always give your problems to God because He will see you
through it
You may have to leave the room or break out in tears
but always remember who you are in Christ and rebuke the evil
spirits
Many people will come against you or not give you credit when it's
due
but always know that it is a test and God will take care of you
We face many obstacles and put on different shoes please always
remember you are the one who make them move
Many times you are misunderstood or monitored much too close
just take a minute to think about what matters the most
Remember who you are in Christ and that the battle is not yours
"We wrestle not against flesh and blood but against principalities,
against the rulers of the darkness of this world against spiritual
wickedness in high places" People are only vessels and it is up to us
by whom we will be used
just know that the trials you face don't have to get the best of you
At times it will be challenging to keep your peace inside just
remember who you are "The eyes of the Lord are upon the
righteous, and his ears are open to their cry"
No matter what you go through and no matter how bad it feels
always put the Lord first and know that He is real.

Ephesians 5:3

But fornication, and all uncleanness, or covetousness,
let it not be once named among you, as becometh saints

The Preachers Wife

Of different faiths we are but to the Lord we are the same
if we continue to carry on this way it will dishonor your name
we love each other it's as clear as can be but where is my ring your
dear wife to be
I understand that you have been scarred and it hurts
but with me as first lady I'm prepared for the worst
We all have pasts that we need to let go so except me as your only
so that what we have will grow
Sweetie I love you and that's without a doubt
but you must make up your mind because our growth you stunt
If it's me that you want then it's Jesus that we need to give us His
blessing and to set us free
I give you this moment to gather your thoughts no pointing
fingers no claiming faults
I give you acceptance to be your wife with reassurance that it's
only me in your life I know that you love me I claim this to be true
but how long must I wait before we say I do?

Matthew 6:24

No man can serve two masters: for either he will hate the one, and love the other: or else he will hold to the one, and despise the other. Ye can not serve God and mammon.

My Brother's Keeper

We have all made choice mistakes but that doesn't mean that we can't give our future a chance

So many times I hear my brothers saying they are not role models because they have done nothing with their lives

but the perfection of man only comes from God

As long as you have breathe in your body you are suppose to learn from your mistakes

but that doesn't mean that it's too late and you can't escape

You are a King that possesses power and strength the devil is someone who you don't need to bargain with

He is the author of all lies and destruction but if you give it to God he will protect you from him

Black men stand up in Jesus name I call you alive from your grave

You don't have to be enslaved to society because "who the son sets free is free indeed" all you have to do is believe

Jesus Christ died for you and me and never meant for us to under achieve

Listen up and put your eyes on God; Satan is trying to corrupt your heart

by dismantling your minds and breaking your faith

give your life to the Lord it is not too late.

John 1: 12

But as many as received Him, to them gave He power to become the sons of God, even to them that believe on His name

Reassurance

"Trust in the Lord with all thine heart, and lean not unto thine own understanding" because growing up in this world can be so demanding

I may not have suffered many of your afflictions, but no matter what you go through Jesus can fix it

Many days of our lives we have been let down by people that we trusted

but if you put your faith in God no man can touch it

"He gives us power to tread on serpents and scorpions and over all the power of the enemy and nothing shall by any means hurt you"

There will be many people who will doubt your success but in the name of Jesus I call you blessed

no weapons formed against you shall prosper God gave me these words so I must spread the gospel

"The blessings of the Lord make it rich and adds no sorrow with it"

so if you didn't get it from God the devil dealt it

"Resist the devil and he will flee", 'cause I can't tell you how many times he ran from me

Repent of your sins and turn away from God no more

because it's not what it looks like it's a spiritual war

as you listen to these words that fill the room please don't forget he will be back soon

he will be looking for no spots or no blemish, so with these words of God let your spirit be quickened.

1 Peter 2:11

Dearly beloved, I beseech you as strangers and pilgrims, abstain from fleshly lusts, which war against the soul

Unity

Favor is deceitful and beauty is vain but a women that fears the Lord she shall be praised

So women don't be deceived keep your eyes on God use the shield of faith it will protect your heart

The man is the head and not the tail but we are the neck to guide him when he turns

The Lord God said it is not good that the man should be alone Bone of his bone, flesh of his flesh, God created women when he put them to rest

He cleaves unto his wife and they shall be one flesh and with the blessings of the Lord no one can attest to this

The blessings of the Lord make it rich and add no sorrow with it marriage is a blessing from God but the devil tries to twist it

What God has joined together let no man put asunder, Exodus 20:17 says "Thou shall not covet"

When a man finds a wife he finds a good thing and obtains favor of the Lord

For this cause shall a man leave his father and his mother and cleave to his wife and they shall both praise the Lord for being in their lives.

Proverbs 22:4

By humility and the fear of the Lord
are riches, and honour, and life.

Someone Special

It's ok to cry when you think nothing is wrong because deep inside
you're feeling alone
 We go through our lives with ambition and much success
 and when we look at our accomplishments we have nothing left
 Love and happiness play a major part in our lives
 but we must acknowledge it and put down our pride
 How can you live and have never been in love this is the greatest
gift that comes from above
 Everyone needs to feel special at some point in our lives
 but we must acknowledge it and put down our pride
 How can you live and have never been in love this is the greatest
gift that comes from above
 Everyone needs to feel special at some point in our lives and when
we don't it dims our shine
 Beautiful woman hold your head up tall because trials and
tribulations come to make you strong
 Whatever is troubling you indeed you must fight because you
cannot hide the truth it is in your eyes
 don't be afraid to call on the Lord he has been waiting for you to
open the door
 believe when I tell you the battle is not yours put your faith in the
Lord Jesus because He has already won.

1 Peter 5:7

Casting all your care upon Him; for He careth for you.

Just A Reminder

"The Lord make it rich and adds no sorrow with it"
pastor you teach this and I am sure Pillar will never forget it
I thank God that you are my Sheppard and when asked I tell the
world that I am a part of your flock
and these words aren't just on paper they are coming from my
heart
I have learned so many things while under your watch and not just
a saying but the meaning of what it was
You are determined that we are obedient but only by enforcing
Gods word
You teach us how to apply the Bible to our every day trials and
tribulations and what I have learned is the closer that I come to
God the devil tries to snatch out and rip apart my heart
and because of his tactics of endless lies and no remorse I must
stay on board with the Lord
"The fruit of the righteous is a tree of life; and he that wins souls is
wise"
"Favor is deceitful and beauty is vain but a woman that fears the
Lord she shall be praised"
First Lady of our pastor with a smile that glows; soft spoken and
gentle with encouraging words to show
I remember when you told me "In many days hence"
At the time I wasn't sure what you meant until the blessings of the
Lord poured down on me quick
Your prayers and your concern have warmed my heart you and the
Pastor are blessings from God.

Psalm 124:8

Our help is in the name of the Lord,
who made heaven and earth.

Faith Works

It amazes me the beauty of God how in the midst of it all He protects my heart
day by day He sends angels into my life
because He wants me to spread His word and tell how He brought me out
He brought me out of a dark place and even though it was dark my path was lit
I could not see ahead of me but from time to time when I looked back I praised the Lord for the enemies attack
The darts that he shot tried to pierce my heart but as I kept my eyes on God I became untouchable
Untouchable to believe anything that the devil tried to present because what God purposed for my life the devil tried to steal
He is the author of lies that I chose not to believe
He is the deceiver that tried to get the best of me
"Get thee behind me Satan you are an offense to me you savor not the things that be of God but those that be of men"
"He was a murderer from the beginning and abides not in the truth, because there is no truth in him."
"When he speaks of a lie he speaks of his own he is a liar and the father of it."
Jesus is real and I put my trust in Him Because God tells us the truth people don't believe Him
"If you have the faith of a mustard seed you can plant a whole harvest" but "faith without works is dead"
Lord I thank you for being my guiding light and for being my eyes when I have no sight
The faith that you have instilled in me is like a roaring storm I will continue to fight until the day you come.

Psalm 34:14

Depart from evil, and do good;
seek peace and pursue it.

The Ways Of The World

Don't be condemned by the ways of the world to every boy and man woman or girl

It's not what it looks like it's just a mirage

I give you this message straight from God

People always wonder what is my test

just look out your window and take your pick

The ways of the world are wicked and cold which demon you'll meet today nobody knows

Some people have the gift to see him when he comes

but he will slip up on you in another form

and when he does you will be amazed and you'll find yourself in a daze

but I can tell you one thing soon I hope to wake up

because of my love for Jesus he can't keep me cuffed

I was so in love with the Lord at the time that I had forgotten Satan wanted my mind

Yes I slipped Satan tricked me well

but not enough to take me to hell

as I am being tried, taunted and teased the Lord still has His hand on me

So Satan I tell you that I live to fight and you will go down with all of Gods might.

Acts 8:22

*Repent therefore of this thy wickedness,
and pray God, if perhaps the thought of
thine heart may be forgiven thee.*

A Cry to the Lord

Stop being a quitter when you haven't even tried

put your faith in the Lord and He will provide

You can't drown out your problems or smoke them away

because when you return things will still be the same

The only way to make it is through Jesus alone

these life situations come to make you strong

Cry, Scream and Shout and let it all out

drop to your knees and scream Jesus please

please, please, please I know that you are real

and I am having trouble being who you called me to be

Lord I need you, I want to be free you said "Ask and you shall receive,"

"I came not to call the righteous but sinners to repentance"

and in recovery they say the first step is admittance

Lord I need you to mend my heart, to make me whole just take control

I need you now to show up and show out to remind the devil that he has no clout

I am a warrior and for you I must fight, these different demons that are in my life "I give unto you power to tread on serpents and scorpions and over all the power of the enemy and nothing shall by any means hurt you"

he means that he has instilled in us the power to fight Satan but only by faith can he be taken

It's time to take a stand for this world that we are in because in due time it is coming to an end

When Jesus comes knocking hurry up and let Him in because between Him and the Devil He is your only friend

Don't leave Him knocking for too long because one day you will look around and He will be gone.

Revelation 6:17

For the great day of His wrath is come;
and who shall be able to stand?

New World Order

We complain about the government and yes they are raping us indeed
 but imagine what it feels like when you can't eat, sleep or be free
Yeah it's true we have chains but some of us have put them on our selves
 Now imagine being a terrorist against a terrorist and each of them is you
 and when you try to remember why you are fighting you haven't got a clue
 From generation to generation but the color stays the same
 and then you turn around and want me to believe that the white man's to
blame for this game!
We've got our men teaching our boys how to be a man
 but when it's time to raise up our families he cannot stand
 We have gotten so caught up in this world that we have taken our eyes off
of God
 so how can He exalt you if you've hardened up your heart?
There are too many people running around here angry and scared
 we have all been hurt, but keeping that pain inside won't change a thing,
because the more you're surrounded by people it's getting harder for you to
breathe;
 with this I'm better than you so you can't be better than me mentality
 There are a lot of people who know the truth and voice their opinions
loud
 but when you start breaking the chains that's when you move the crowd!
 I have gotten older and I see more and so I hear lots of things
 but how come no one can tell me why Martin Luther was our only King?
We look at our ancestors and how they have paved the way
 but when you look at our generation there is nothing we can say
Everyone is caught up in this modern way of life
 we have turned our backs not realizing we are all under turmoil and strife
When will we unite and extend our hands to our own
 but first it begins with God because earth wasn't meant to be our home
You can question and you can judge and wonder where is God,
 but when you are given pointers on how to find Him some just smile and
nod
 you have to come to realize that the first change is within

because it's time to start making our enemies our friends
and this can't be done if God isn't in the midst
We are uneducated about our rights and the ones who know have yet
to tell
and then we ask the question why so many of our black men are in jail
It's been time to stand! While everyone has a seat
and when we look for someone to go on the front line you hear not
me, not me
We all have the power to make things change, but people spend more
energy using the Lords name in vain
He is my chief so I must take His orders; The Devils government is
coming announcing the birth of the New World Order.

Galatians 6:2

Bear ye one anothers burdens, and
so fulfill the law of Christ.

Reflections

When you wake up in the morning there is a smile on your face
is it because you know Jesus loves you or because you have lost
some weight?
When you go out and face the world are you blessing others in the
process or are you being what is called an Angel reject?
When you tell people you love them is it because it is true
or are you thinking of ways that it benefits you?
When someone tells you their needs do you give to bless or do you
give just to stick out your chest?
When you see someone in trouble do you bow your head and pray
or do you spread their business for the next few days?
When you live to see another year do you thank God that you are
here or do you just say cheers and have another beer?
Even though it is hard to abstain from sin
everyone has a piece of God within
let Him come alive inside you because unlike the devil Jesus will
never lie to you
And if in any way this has touched your heart it is never too late to
get right with God
repent of your sins and ask God to forgive because serving the
Lord is the only way to live.

Psalm 92:2

To shew forth thy loving kindness in the morning, and thy faithfulness every night

What You Mean To Me

I have always wanted to express my sincere thanks as I thank God
for blessing me with this Pillar Of Truth saint

Many days and many nights in that season of my life you extended
your ear to me

I have called you early in the morning before the sun rose and late
at night

No matter what time it was you out poured your light

In the midst of my confusion and in the midst of my pain you
reassured me that everything would be all right, in Jesus name

You quoted scriptures and gave me the word you even understood
all of my hurts

I never knew the true friend that we have in the Lord; but I thank
you for guiding me into His loving arms

I may not call you as much now but I love you the same

just consider that assignment done in Jesus name

I thank God for your strength at the time when I was weak

because His word in you breathed the life back into me

Recently you told me the Lord didn't give me the spirit of fear

so stop fighting Him when He is trying to come in

I thank you Lord for this women of God

and I ask you to bestow your blessings on her from my heart

When I first came to Pillar you would praise the Lord loud

then one day I looked up you sat silently in the crowd

but I thank God for your deliverance you have been set free

and "who the Son sets free is free indeed."

What you mean to me is more than just these words

but verbally they pour out from my heart to yours.

Matthew 7:7

Ask, and it shall be given you: seek, and ye shall find: knock and it shall be opened unto you

A Question

I don't know why this is happening all I know is that it is
the Lord gives me strength and that is how I live
He loves me throughout the times I put my back against the wall
but even in my sorrow I find the strength to call
Jesus I am hurting can you take away the pain?
He answers yes because Lord is my name
Jesus I am confused can you give me a peace of mind?
As soon as I asked that question he came right on time
Jesus I am weak can you give me strength?
In a moments time my head was unbent
of all the things he has done for you won't you dedicate your life to
praising his name and spreading the word
because haven't you heard Jesus is Lord?

Matthew 24:13

But he that shall endure unto the end shall be saved.

Stand Up

I just want to be heard; my voice, my poetry, my story, my life

Do you know what it's like to be out here on your own with no keys to a place that we call home?

Do you understand the concept of faith its' self?

Something that can't be wavered no matter how you felt.

Do you understand the true meaning of being a child of God?

if so tell me your life so that I can feel your scars.

Do you know what it's like to turn the other cheek?

Well I do because every side of me has been beat.

Do you understand the true meaning of a spiritual warfare?

Because "we walk in the flesh we do not war after the flesh the weapons of our warfare are not carnal but mighty through God to the pulling down of strong holds casting down imaginations and every high thing that exalts its self against the knowledge of God."

When God wants your attention He has His way of getting it

but what we have to do is receive it

receive the fact that He is Lord

and "all things are possible through Christ Jesus" that's what he died for

Call Him what you want what's in a name

but when you get through calling Him; His power is still the same

It was no accident that we were born and are living in these trying times

"He has saved us and called us with a holy calling not according to our works but according to His own purpose and grace"

but somewhere along the line we let the devil in and most of us enjoy living in sin. Well people of God it's time to stand up

so put on your whole armor and let's give the devil the flux.

Psalms 91:3

Surely He shall deliver thee from the snare of the fowler, and from the noisome pestilence.

Satan's Web

Got caught up in the web he weaved
crying asking God to take Satan's hands off me cause I want to be free
free of the apple that Adam gave me
cause every bite was delicious fulfilling me
I was deceived; so the Pastor said
spiritually speaking it hadn't sank in to my head
Sister you don't know the power that you posses
that's why Satan's coming at you with all his best
you are a women of God don't take Satan's devices to your heart
My soul has been touched; and it doesn't hurt as much as what I'm use to
I don't cry as much, as I use to, 2006 you don't know what I been
through
He said because the Lord is in process of using you I was confused
You see the Devil plants traps to block your blessings
and before you know it you are being tested
don't ever think that you are above the law
the laws of the land and the laws of the spirit
because the devil will tempt you with something wicked
If you have the faith of a mustard seed you can plant a whole harvest
but at the same time ask for the blood of Jesus to guard it
When I bit that apple I swallowed a seed
and for the rest of my life it's embedded in me
and times I can't breathe and times I can't sleep
and my flesh is weak so I drop to my knees cause I'm in need of a fix
my heart is aching and my souls crying out
as help me Jesus flows from my mouth
tears flow from my face as I envision Adams face
but I must pick up my cross and take my rightful place
It's a war zone, my flesh says yes and my spirit says no
with all of this pulling it's hard to let go
Psalms 51 I use like a gun, my heart is racing Satan can't overcome
I am a warrior and I must fight Ephesians 6:11 and 12 saves my life.

41

Galatians 5:1

Stand fast therefore in the liberty wherewith Christ hath made us free, and be not entangled again with the yoke of bondage.

Through The Pain

Love each other through the pain because we have eternity to gain
both God fearing people trying to find our way
feelings are caught up as this love cannot stay
it feels so good to be heard and understood
but if this isn't your season then what season would
allow us to be free without sinning against God
Because the love that I feel is a legend for my past
so I ask myself this question how long will it last
being so high just pumps my adrenaline
being so high allows me to feel again
Ice cold as my inner man says
What is the velocity to feeling some ones love for me
something that feels so good feels so bad a love that I never knew I
could have
from the beginning it seemed like a mirage
thinking to myself is this from God
The Devils got it twisted this is my fate he will not defeat
although I am going through changes the Lord has his hand on me
My heart hurts every day as it pumps with passion
my heart hurts every day is this everlasting
When I look in your eyes I can feel your spirit too hard to escape just
can't bare it the way you caress my face relaxes my mind calms my
spirit
I've grown to realize that every season is for a reason
but in this season was a storm of emotions
rocking the boat but it kept on coasting
never bragging or boasting just mind blowing
didn't know if I was coming or going
couldn't focus on daily tasks, kind of like I was in a trance
no control just moving to the flow which way I was going I didn't even
know
At times I found myself at a stand still trying to hear a word from
God

Although I knew He was there at times it was hard
I never knew a feeling like this existed out of all these years
how could I have missed this
Unique and rare everything I have ever wanted living there
it's all a lot for me to bare
caught off guard it was all unexpected
the Devil crept in but Jesus kept it
my soul, my spirit, my peace of mind
he even gave me the words to right these lines
because this story that I tell is not only mine.

Psalms 119:101

I have refrained my feet from every evil way, that I might keep thy word.

My Heart

I wanted you to rescue me but I was afraid of being hurt
and if I am not doing it for God then what is it worth?
I love you I can't lie because it's a part of being real
so I have chosen this time to tell you how I feel
When I look into your eyes I enter the window to your soul
and there I get a chance to explore the unknown
a galaxy of unconditional love and when I get there I forget where
I'm from
I'm not trying to escape things or block anything out
so I find myself praying to God to help me out
I ask him to give me understanding of this journey that I am on
and what is the purpose of me being in love?
What do I do with it if I must keep it to myself?
Because I don't think I could feel this way for anyone else
I'm not questioning its authencity because the mold has already
been broken
and from you I have received more than just a token
A "Living Legend" you proclaim and you are indeed
but what would your legend be like if it included me?
I may never know 'cause at times you seem cold
and given our history what does the future hold?
Sometimes I am uncertain of what you really feel
like if you're angry at me for my life given deals
You shelter your heart it makes me nervous when I can't feel
it leaves me feeling like it's another "raw deal"
Maybe I'm too emotional for someone of your class
Time keeps ticking how long will this last?
Don't jump to conclusions I'm not angry or upset
I'm simply telling you what's going on inside of my head
I know my life is complicated but I took what I was given
so with my "Faith in God" I will keep on living
Sometimes I feel like a baby because I'm new to this all
but who's there to catch me at times when I fall?

Jesus, I know; but he also uses people.
But in my life there aren't many they have become feeble
Certain things happen in our lives and we develop bonds
but I just can't figure out whose side I'm on
People have a tendency to do what they think is right
without the knowledge of knowing how it affects someone's life
Regardless of the facts, I think of you as a friend
and with the gift of poetry that will never end.

Psalm 127:3

Lo, children are an heritage of the Lord: and the fruit of the womb is His reward.

God's Angels

Sometimes your heart gets troubled and questions begin to arise
you begin to wonder and ask God why
Well I don't know the answer because I ask why myself
but God foresaw our future and only wants to bring us wealth
We have suffered many losses all precious and dear
some lives were taken and some weren't meant to be here
To the twins mommy loves you and will see you when I come
home
because it's now I know that you belonged to God
Although I have never held you I've seen you in my dreams
and you both were as beautiful as I imagined you to be
It hurts daily to have endured such a loss
but I give an honor to God because of your lives he paid the cost
No I am not bitter to the tragedy its self
just at the fact of knowing that you were never held
and even still it wouldn't have been easier to have said goodbye
just wanted you to know that we loved you
and gave you a kiss goodnight.

2 Timothy 4:7

*I have fought a good fight, I have finished
my course, I have kept the faith.*

The Whole Armor

When things around you seem as though they were falling apart
and you feel like Jesus has left you when times have gotten hard
When your children and your husband are all acting strange
When everything goes wrong you're the one to blame
When you're almost about to lose your mind
you want to give up and you keep on crying
When you can't sleep from thinking
and can't think from being sleep
this is the point when the devil thinks he got you beat
When you see what you see and you know what you know
and a person tells you you're losing you're glow
When the devil tried to shield your eyes
When the devil tried to make food be despised
When the devil tried to make you fall asleep behind that wheel
When the devil tried to steal your joy
When the devil tried to confuse your every thought
When the devil kept on roaming your house
When through it all you found your way loose
'cause you kept your eyes on Jesus because He is the truth
When you said Satan I see you and you must flee
because I know that the Lord has His hand on me
When you cried and repented to Jesus our Lord
When He sent His angels you pulled out that sword
When you bowed your head before God and slipped on that breast
plate
you said Jesus is Lord and you kept on pressing
When you stood on solid ground and held up that shield
that was when you used your faith to prevail
When you put on that helmet and knocked the devil out
all the ambassadors of Christ screamed and shout
People of God I know that you are listening
the devil is a liar and you must keep on pressing.

Romans 8:31

What shall we then say to these things? If God be for us, who can be against us?

Still Standing

When God gets through dealing with you it's then you will know that
heaven is the only place for you
"Whom He loveth He chastens but if He doesn't chastise you; you are a
bastard and are not His son"
2006 was a rough one, a battle with this and a battle with that
but through it all God had my back
Sleepless nights with the Bible by my side
the demons were coming but my faith did not slide
It ignited the flame to call out Jesus' name
and every time I called He came
He sent his Angels they surrounded me day by day
as I walked that walk of faith
"A substance of things not seen but hoped for"
another year 2007 it's finally here
As I stood there watching the fireworks from my face ran tears
as I began to thank the Lord for getting me through to see another year
Seven means completion and now I am feeling whole
so any one running on empty I encourage you to fill up on the Lord
He will fill you with completion in the middle of a storm
but when you go through that storm you must have God
He gives you the "power to tread on serpents and scorpions and over all
the power of the enemy and nothing shall by any means hurt you"
Don't be afraid to stand up against the enemy
because he is really weak, a liar, a killer and nothing but a thief
All of the demons tremble when I walk into a room
because with the power of God in me they know that I rule
Every time I said I don't want to do that anymore I want to be right
Satan came at me with all of his might
Throwing darts and even had the nerve to dig me a ditch
but in my heart I know that he can't win
"The righteous cry and the Lord hears and delivers them out of all their
troubles" He will save you because you can't save yourself
That's why I am glad that Jesus wept.

Psalm 126:5

They that sow in tears shall reap in joy.

Deliverance

Some people refer to poetry as an art
But I refer to it as words from my heart
And with these words I have developed a bond
My heart bonds with scriptures to provide a clearer picture
To discover and uncover what the Lord requires of me
To tell that I was held captive and how the Lord set me free
I have been referred to as the female Job
So everything that I have lost I am believing God for it
"Every word of God is pure He is a shield unto them that put their
trust in Him," so I take my problems and I rest in Him
When the enemy comes up against me I give my best to Him
He said "The weapons of our warfare are not carnal but mighty
through God to the pulling down of strong holds"
Then I began to "cast down imaginations and every high thing that
exalts its self against the knowledge of God
Bringing into captivity every thought to the obedience of Christ"
Because I have been chosen the devil wants to take my life
And I thank God for my pastor for giving me more knowledge of Christ
Because without Gods power Satan would rule my life
You see I don't have to think twice about serving the Lord
Because I've been on the other side at Satan's door
I didn't have to knock he maliciously invited me in
He wanted me to think that everything that I loved was my friend
He wanted me to think that if I indulged in sin that my problems
would end
But little did I know that's when my test began
I am a walking testimony of the goodness of God
I am a walking testimony of sin in my heart
Indulging in temptation feeling the flames from Satan's pit
The Lord was with me the whole time so I didn't quit
I didn't give up I was confused I can't lie
Because if what I was doing was so wrong how could it feel so right?
"The righteous cries and the Lord hears and delivers them of all their
troubles".

Printed in the United States
110066LV00005B/67/P